CGP hatches a Handwriting plan for spring!

It's crucial to keep working on Handwriting skills throughout Year 4, and this CGP book is a brilliant way to keep pupils practising regularly...

It's packed with fun, engaging exercises for every day of the spring term, covering all the words they'll need to use most often.

We've included plenty of full sentences and paragraphs to tackle too — perfect for helping them build up their fluency and confidence!

What CGP is all about

Our sole aim here at CGP is to produce the highest quality books — carefully written, immaculately presented and dangerously close to being funny.

Then we work our socks off to get them out to you — at the cheapest possible prices.

Contents

☑ Use the tick boxes to help keep a record of which pages have been attempted.

Week 1
- ☑ Day 1 1
- ☑ Day 2 2
- ☑ Day 3 3
- ☑ Day 4 4
- ☑ Day 5 5

Week 2
- ☑ Day 1 6
- ☑ Day 2 7
- ☑ Day 3 8
- ☑ Day 4 9
- ☑ Day 5 10

Week 3
- ☑ Day 1 11
- ☑ Day 2 12
- ☑ Day 3 13
- ☑ Day 4 14
- ☑ Day 5 15

Week 4
- ☑ Day 1 16
- ☑ Day 2 17
- ☑ Day 3 18
- ☑ Day 4 19
- ☑ Day 5 20

Week 5
- ☑ Day 1 21
- ☑ Day 2 22
- ☑ Day 3 23
- ☑ Day 4 24
- ☑ Day 5 25

Week 6
- ☑ Day 1 26
- ☑ Day 2 27
- ☑ Day 3 28
- ☑ Day 4 29
- ☑ Day 5 30

Week 7
- ☑ Day 1 31
- ☑ Day 2 32
- ☑ Day 3 33
- ☑ Day 4 34
- ☑ Day 5 35

Week 8
- ☑ Day 1 36
- ☑ Day 2 37
- ☑ Day 3 38
- ☑ Day 4 39
- ☑ Day 5 40

Week 9
- [✓] Day 1 41
- [✓] Day 2 42
- [✓] Day 3 43
- [✓] Day 4 44
- [✓] Day 5 45

Week 10
- [✓] Day 1 46
- [✓] Day 2 47
- [✓] Day 3 48
- [✓] Day 4 49
- [✓] Day 5 50

Week 11
- [✓] Day 1 51
- [✓] Day 2 52
- [✓] Day 3 53
- [✓] Day 4 54
- [✓] Day 5 55

Week 12
- [✓] Day 1 56
- [✓] Day 2 57
- [✓] Day 3 58
- [✓] Day 4 59
- [✓] Day 5 60

Published by CGP

ISBN: 978 1 78908 665 2

Editors: Rachel Craig-McFeely, Mary Falkner, Rob Hayman, Sharon Keeley-Holden and Camilla Sheridan.

With thanks to Alison Griffin and Ellen Burton for the proofreading.
With thanks to Emily Smith for the copyright research.

Printed by Elanders Ltd, Newcastle upon Tyne.
Clipart on the cover and throughout the book from Corel®
Images used on pages 18, 19 and 20 © www.edu-clips.com
Based on the classic CGP style created by Richard Parsons.

Text, design, layout and original illustrations © Coordination Group Publications Ltd. (CGP) 2020
All rights reserved.

Photocopying this book is not permitted, even if you have a CLA licence.
Extra copies are available from CGP with next day delivery • 0800 1712 712 • www.cgpbooks.co.uk

How to Use this Book

- This book contains 60 pages of daily handwriting practice.
- It's split into 12 sections — that's roughly one section for each week of the Year 4 Spring term.
- A week is made up of 5 pages, so there's one for every school day of the term (Monday – Friday).
- Each page should take about 10 minutes to complete.
- Each week, pupils practise copying individual words, such as spelling words from the National Curriculum, then whole sentences and paragraphs with a particular theme. This helps them to build up their handwriting fluency.
- A typical page looks something like this:

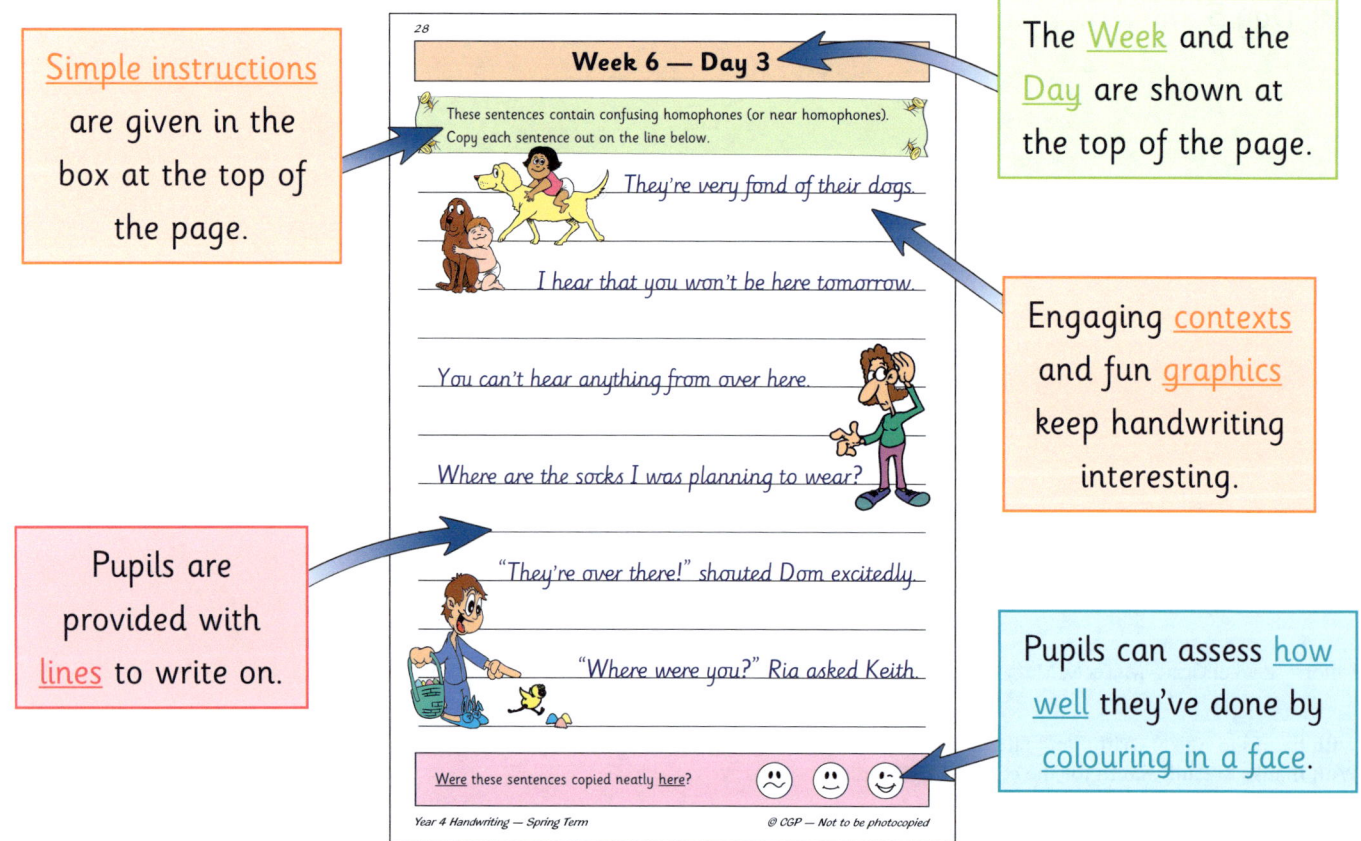

If you are a parent or guardian using this book at home with your child, you should bear in mind that different schools have different handwriting styles. You should check with the school to see how they write and join each letter. Some schools also have different break letters (letters that don't join to the next letter). For example, 'g' can be a break letter or can be joined. You should check which break letters the school uses.

Week 1 — Day 1

These words all end with a suffix. Sometimes the letter before the suffix is doubled and sometimes it isn't. Copy each word three times.

listening

gardener

opened

offering

happened

revealed

traveller

forbidden

beginning

controlled

forgetting

propeller

Did you manage to copy each word neatly?

Week 1 — Day 2

Copy each of these sentences neatly.

My favourite possession is my shiny silver bicycle.

Bev got ready for the special occasion.

 Boris couldn't remember the question, but he was certain it was important.

Sadly, Stu realised that he should have chosen a different material for the bar.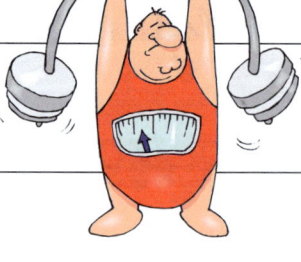

How did you get on with these sentences?

Week 1 — Day 3

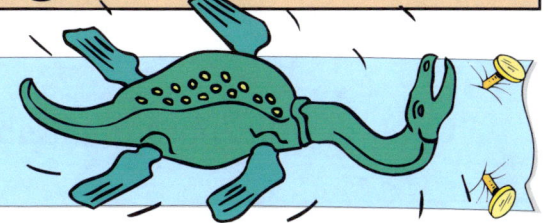

Copy these exciting facts about plesiosaurs.

Plesiosaurs lived at the same time as dinosaurs.

They were giant reptiles that lived in the sea.

The biggest plesiosaurs were about 14 metres long.

Many plesiosaurs had very long necks.

They swam using their four big flippers.

They ate other sea creatures, like squid and fish.

Did you copy these sentences out neatly?

Week 1 — Day 4

Copy out this paragraph about a famous monster.

The Loch Ness Monster, or Nessie as she's also known, is said to live in Loch Ness in Scotland. Reports of a strange creature in the loch can be traced back to ancient times. However, scientists believe that Nessie is just a myth. One explanation is that people have spotted giant eels in the loch.

How well did you do today?

Week 1 — Day 5

Copy this account of a sighting of the Loch Ness Monster.

This morning, I was walking my dog, Buster, along the loch shore. Suddenly, the mist cleared, and a shape rose out of the water. Buster spotted it too and growled fiercely. The creature's neck was like an elephant's trunk. As it dived back under the water, I glimpsed a paddle-like flipper.

How neat is your handwriting today?

Week 2 — Day 1

The words below end with the suffix 'ation'.
Copy them each out twice.

admiration

application

destination

education

exploration

fascination

motivation

information

donation

preparation

sensation

translation

How well did you do today?

Week 2 — Day 2

Here are some sentences that contain words with the suffix 'ation'. Have a go at copying them out.

The coach shouted in frustration.

Alan always appreciated alliteration.

Karabo went shopping for Christmas decorations.

Kat preferred books with illustrations.

Zach is hopping with anticipation.

The writer was lacking inspiration for her story.

Will your handwriting be met with admir<u>ation</u>?

Week 2 — Day 3

Copy out the sentences on the lines below.

Early in the morning, Hattie went to the library.

I can't imagine a stranger, more peculiar creature.

Sam often keeps his promises.

After the lesson ended, the enthusiastic teacher continued describing the island at length.

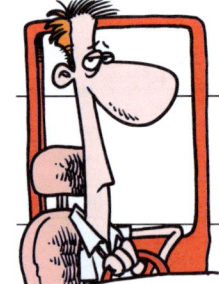

"We'll probably arrive soon," said my Dad.

Was your handwriting neat on this page?

Week 2 — Day 4

Read the fable below, then copy it out.

The mice were discussing how to outwit the cat. One said that they should attach a bell to the cat so that they knew when he was coming. However, a wise old mouse asked, "Who will put the bell on the cat?" The moral is: impossible solutions don't help to solve problems.

Could you copy this fable fantastically?

Week 2 — Day 5

Here is a fact file about carnivorous plants. Copy it out neatly.

Carnivorous plants eat animals such as insects. They catch their prey in many ways. Pitcher plants trick insects into falling into a pool of digestive fluid. Sundew plants have sticky leaves which insects get caught on. Venus flytraps snap shut when touched.

Did you copy out this information correctly?

Week 3 — Day 1

These words each have an '-ly' suffix.
Copy each word out three times.

sadly

mostly

usually

silently

originally

ghostly

weekly

famously

completely

hopefully

musically

finally

Did you do brilliantly with today's words?

Week 3 — Day 2

Copy out these sentences with apostrophes.

The girl's hat fell off in the girls' toilets.

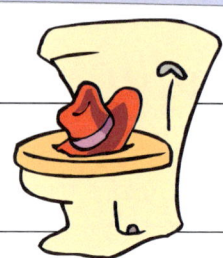

The baby's painting was better than the other babies' paintings.

The dog's bark was scarier than the lions' roars.

The baker's cake was tastier than the other bakers'.

How did you get on with these sentences?

Week 3 — Day 3

Here are four facts about the Ancient Olympics for you to copy.

The Ancient Olympics were invented in Olympia, Greece, over 2700 years ago.

Events included running, long jump and javelin.

Most athletes competed naked, although there was a race run with a helmet and shield.

Wrestlers covered themselves in oil before fighting.

Do you deserve a gold medal for your writing?

Week 3 — Day 4

Copy out this paragraph about the modern Olympics.

The modern Olympics started in Athens in 1896. They are held every four years and are hosted by a different country each time. At the 2016 Olympics in Rio de Janeiro, there were over 11 000 athletes from 207 countries competing. The UK has hosted the Olympics three times.

 Were you able to copy this paragraph?

Week 3 — Day 5

Here is a paragraph about an incredible Paralympian. Copy it out below.

Trischa Zorn is the most decorated Paralympian in history. She won 55 medals for swimming across seven Paralympics, including 41 gold medals. She was born blind, but swam alongside sighted swimmers from the age of 10. She won her final medal in 2004, 24 years after her first one.

Did your copying go swimmingly?

Week 4 — Day 1

All of the words on this page end in 'ly'. Copy them out three times.

happily

sleepily

angrily

heavily

luckily

nobly

hungrily

gently

simply

humbly

miserably

wiggly

How did you get on with these 'ly' words?

Week 4 — Day 2

These sentences contain words that end in 'ly'.
Copy out each sentence.

Edwin yawned lazily as he got out of bed.

The farmer sighed as the wriggly pig escaped again.

Incredibly, she climbed the crumbly cliff.

Isha grumpily let her brother win the game.

The bear looked fierce, but she was actually very cuddly.

How did you do with these sentences?

Week 4 — Day 3

Copy out these fabulous facts about dinosaurs.

Dinosaurs were reptiles that lived on Earth, but became extinct around sixty-six million years ago. The smallest dinosaur is thought to have been smaller than a hummingbird, while the tallest was eighteen metres tall. That's the height of four double-decker buses!

Did you copy the facts out neatly?

Week 4 — Day 4

Here's a paragraph about a famous fossil collector called Mary Anning. Read it, then copy it out below.

Born in 1799, Mary spent lots of her childhood searching for fossils on the Jurassic Coast in Dorset. When she was 12, Mary discovered the fossilised remains of a 200 million year old reptile! She went on to discover many more amazing fossils. Some are displayed in the Natural History Museum.

How did you get on with this page?

Week 4 — Day 5

The text below is from a newspaper article. Copy it out carefully.

Class 4B made an incredible discovery on a trip to the beach to look at rock pools. "At first I thought it was a dog's paw print, but then I realised it was far too big!" said nine year old Li. Scientists believe the print belonged to a dinosaur that walked the Earth 130 million years ago.

Is your copy of the paragraph neat?

Week 5 — Day 1

Copy each word twice across the page.

comically

basically

typically

magically

physically

frantically

dramatically

mechanically

robotically

wholly

truly

duly

How did you get on with these words?

Week 5 — Day 2

Copy each of these sentences on the line below.

"It's the worst day ever," he said dramatically.

Mum shouted frantically, "Where are my keys?"

Sue shouted, "Got you at last!" gleefully.

Cautiously, Ola whispered, "I think it is safe now."

Mrs Smith angrily told the children to stop ringing her doorbell and running away.

How neatly did you copy these sentences?

Week 5 — Day 3

Copy the fascinating facts about owls below.

Owls are nocturnal so they are active at night.

Mostly, owls eat insects, small mammals and birds.

They catch their prey with amazingly strong talons.

Owls fly silently, so their prey doesn't hear them.

An owl's feathers help it to camouflage.

The name for a group of owls is a parliament.

How well did you manage today?

Week 5 — Day 4

Copy this paragraph about some problems faced by owls.

Owls are powerful predators, but there are lots of threats to their existence. Areas of rough grassland are decreasing. Lots of animals that owls eat live there, so this means less food for owls. Also, owls nest in hollow trees, and as these are removed there are fewer places for owls to raise their owlets.

How neatly did you copy this paragraph?

Week 5 — Day 5

Copy the beginning of this famous poem by Edward Lear.

The Owl and the Pussy-cat went to sea

In a beautiful pea-green boat,

They took some honey, and plenty of money,

Wrapped up in a five-pound note.

The Owl looked up to the stars above,

And sang to a small guitar.

How well did you copy this bit of poetry?

Week 6 — Day 1

Homophones are words that sound the same, but are spelt differently and mean different things. Copy out each word three times.

air

heir

affect

effect

desert

dessert

aloud

allowed

aisle

isle

herd

heard

How well did you copy out these homophones?

Week 6 — Day 2

Here are some sentences containing pairs of homophones. Have a go at copying them out.

The prophet predicted he would make lots of profit.

 I wonder whether the weather will be fine.

Olivia couldn't have guessed who the guest was.

Dean is a serial cereal-eater.

Kwame spent a morning mourning his lost biscuit.

 The whole car fell into a huge hole.

Did you copy these sentences neatly?

Week 6 — Day 3

These sentences contain confusing homophones (or near homophones). Copy each sentence out on the line below.

They're very fond of their dogs.

I hear that you won't be here tomorrow.

You can't hear anything from over here.

Where are the socks I was planning to wear?

"They're over there!" shouted Dom excitedly.

"Where were you?" Ria asked Keith.

Were these sentences copied neatly here?

Week 5 — Day 1

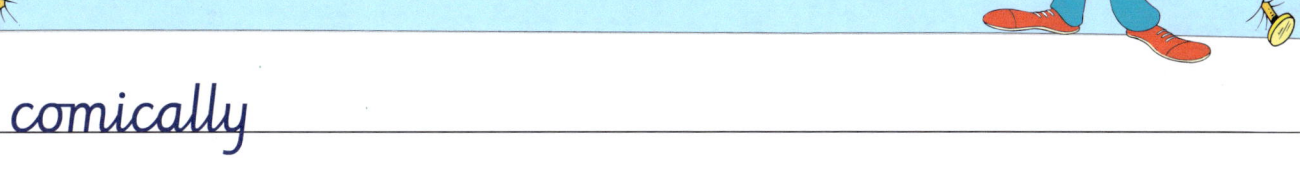

Copy each word twice across the page.

comically

basically

typically

magically

physically

frantically

dramatically

mechanically

robotically

wholly

truly

duly

How did you get on with these words?

Week 5 — Day 2

Copy each of these sentences on the line below.

"It's the worst day ever," he said dramatically.

Mum shouted frantically, "Where are my keys?"

Sue shouted, "Got you at last!" gleefully.

Cautiously, Ola whispered, "I think it is safe now."

Mrs Smith angrily told the children to stop ringing her doorbell and running away.

How neatly did you copy these sentences?

Week 5 — Day 3

Copy the fascinating facts about owls below.

Owls are nocturnal so they are active at night.

Mostly, owls eat insects, small mammals and birds.

They catch their prey with amazingly strong talons.

Owls fly silently, so their prey doesn't hear them.

An owl's feathers help it to camouflage.

The name for a group of owls is a parliament.

How well did you manage today?

Week 5 — Day 4

Copy this paragraph about some problems faced by owls.

Owls are powerful predators, but there are lots of threats to their existence. Areas of rough grassland are decreasing. Lots of animals that owls eat live there, so this means less food for owls. Also, owls nest in hollow trees, and as these are removed there are fewer places for owls to raise their owlets.

How neatly did you copy this paragraph?

Week 5 — Day 5

Copy the beginning of this famous poem by Edward Lear.

The Owl and the Pussy-cat went to sea

In a beautiful pea-green boat,

They took some honey, and plenty of money,

Wrapped up in a five-pound note.

The Owl looked up to the stars above,

And sang to a small guitar.

How well did you copy this bit of poetry?

Week 6 — Day 1

Homophones are words that sound the same, but are spelt differently and mean different things. Copy out each word three times.

air

heir

affect

effect

desert

dessert

aloud

allowed

aisle

isle

herd

heard

How well did you copy out these homophones?

Week 6 — Day 2

Here are some sentences containing pairs of homophones. Have a go at copying them out.

The prophet predicted he would make lots of profit.

I wonder whether the weather will be fine.

Olivia couldn't have guessed who the guest was.

Dean is a serial cereal-eater.

Kwame spent a morning mourning his lost biscuit.

The whole car fell into a huge hole.

Did you copy these sentences neatly?

Week 6 — Day 3

These sentences contain confusing homophones (or near homophones). Copy each sentence out on the line below.

They're very fond of their dogs.

I hear that you won't be here tomorrow.

You can't hear anything from over here.

Where are the socks I was planning to wear?

"They're over there!" shouted Dom excitedly.

"Where were you?" Ria asked Keith.

Were these sentences copied neatly here?

Week 6 — Day 4

Read this script about a shopping mix-up, then copy it out below.

Priya: Jack, did you get me the flour from the shop?

Jack: Yes, it's over there, on the table.

Priya: I can't see any — there's just a daisy.

Jack: Well, a daisy is a type of flower…

Priya: I asked you for flour, not a flower! How can I bake brownies with a daisy?

Was your copying better than Jack's shopping?

Week 6 — Day 5

Here are some homophone jokes. Read them, then copy them out.

What did the stag say when his friend tripped over? — "Oh deer!"

What did one sheep say to the other? — "I love ewe."

"How would you like your steak?" asked the waiter. "Roar," replied the lion.

Did you copy these puns purr-fectly?

Week 7 — Day 1

Copy out the names of the seven continents and five oceans on Earth.

Atlantic Ocean   Arctic Ocean

North America   Europe   Asia

Pacific Ocean

Africa

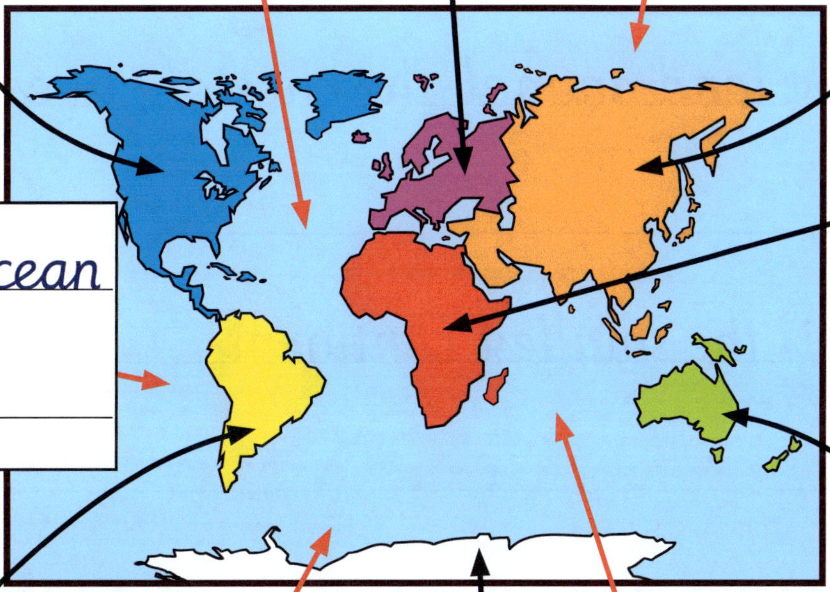

Southern Ocean   Indian Ocean

South America   Antarctica   Oceania

Did you neatly copy these geographical words?

Week 7 — Day 2

Copy out these facts about six of the continents.

Mount Everest, Earth's tallest mountain, is in Asia.

The world's largest rainforest is in South America.

The fastest land animal, the cheetah, lives in Africa.

Oceania is the smallest continent.

Europeans eat more chocolate than anyone else.

T-Rexes and Triceratops lived in North America.

How well did you write these facts?

Week 7 — Day 3

Copy out the names of the seven continents and five oceans on Earth.

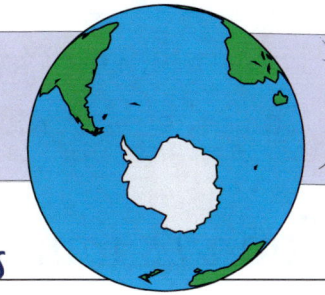

Antarctica is the continent which lies around the Earth's South Pole. It is the only continent where no people live permanently. Antarctica is the world's largest desert as it is usually too cold for rain. It is mostly covered in ice and is home to several species of penguin.

How did you do with these Antarctic facts?

Week 7 — Day 4

Here is an entry from the diary of an Antarctic explorer. Copy the paragraph out below.

Today's journey has been incredibly difficult for us. We have had to make camp as the blizzard was only getting heavier. As I write, the snow is building up around our tent and we have had to bring the sled dogs inside to keep us warm. Tomorrow, we start our final trek to the South Pole.

Did you write this diary entry neatly?

Week 7 — Day 5

Below are important instructions for planning an Antarctic adventure. Read them, then carefully copy them out.

Make sure you have packed plenty of warm clothes as it will get extremely cold. Next, check that there is lots of food for you and your sled dogs. Make sure that you've packed your tent, as well as an extra cosy sleeping bag. Finally, remember your skis! You'll definitely need them!

How did you get on with these sentences?

Week 8 — Day 1

Vowel sounds can be tricky to spell. The 'y' in the words below is pronounced like the 'i' in 'bin'. Copy them out three times.

crystal

Egypt

gym

hymn

lyric

mystery

myth

physics

pyramid

symbol

syrup

typical

Did you write these words out neatly?

Week 6 — Day 4

Read this script about a shopping mix-up, then copy it out below.

Priya: Jack, did you get me the flour from the shop?

Jack: Yes, it's over there, on the table.

Priya: I can't see any — there's just a daisy.

Jack: Well, a daisy is a type of flower...

Priya: I asked you for flour, not a flower!

How can I bake brownies with a daisy?

Was your copying better than Jack's shopping?

Week 6 — Day 5

Here are some homophone jokes. Read them, then copy them out.

What did the stag say when his friend tripped over? — "Oh deer!"

What did one sheep say to the other? — "I love ewe."

"How would you like your steak?" asked the waiter. "Roar," replied the lion.

Did you copy these puns purr-fectly?

Week 7 — Day 1

Copy out the names of the seven continents and five oceans on Earth.

Atlantic Ocean

Arctic Ocean

North America

Europe

Asia

Pacific Ocean

Africa

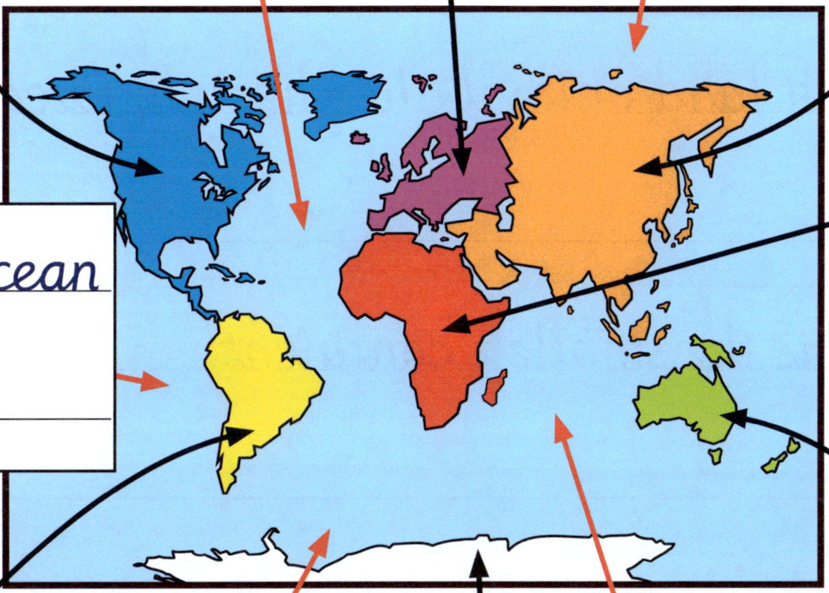

Southern Ocean

Indian Ocean

South America

Antarctica

Oceania

Did you neatly copy these geographical words?

Week 7 — Day 2

Copy out these facts about six of the continents.

Mount Everest, Earth's tallest mountain, is in Asia.

The world's largest rainforest is in South America.

The fastest land animal, the cheetah, lives in Africa.

Oceania is the smallest continent.

Europeans eat more chocolate than anyone else.

T-Rexes and Triceratops lived in North America.

How well did you write these facts?

Week 7 — Day 3

Copy out the names of the seven continents and five oceans on Earth.

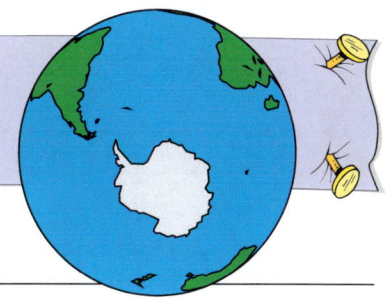

Antarctica is the continent which lies around the Earth's South Pole. It is the only continent where no people live permanently. Antarctica is the world's largest desert as it is usually too cold for rain. It is mostly covered in ice and is home to several species of penguin.

How did you do with these Antarctic facts?

Week 7 — Day 4

Here is an entry from the diary of an Antarctic explorer. Copy the paragraph out below.

Today's journey has been incredibly difficult for us. We have had to make camp as the blizzard was only getting heavier. As I write, the snow is building up around our tent and we have had to bring the sled dogs inside to keep us warm. Tomorrow, we start our final trek to the South Pole.

Did you write this diary entry neatly?

Week 7 — Day 5

Below are important instructions for planning an Antarctic adventure. Read them, then carefully copy them out.

Make sure you have packed plenty of warm clothes as it will get extremely cold. Next, check that there is lots of food for you and your sled dogs. Make sure that you've packed your tent, as well as an extra cosy sleeping bag. Finally, remember your skis! You'll definitely need them!

How did you get on with these sentences?

Week 8 — Day 1

Vowel sounds can be tricky to spell. The 'y' in the words below is pronounced like the 'i' in 'bin'. Copy them out three times.

crystal

Egypt

gym

hymn

lyric

mystery

myth

physics

pyramid

symbol

syrup

typical

Did you write these words out neatly?

Week 8 — Day 2

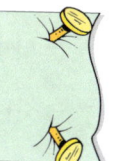

Read these sentences about Ancient Egypt, then copy them out.

Ancient Egyptians lived thousands of years ago.

They built towns around the River Nile in Africa.

Ancient Egyptian rulers were called pharaohs.

They wrote in symbols called hieroglyphs.

They preserved the bodies of important people through mummification.

Is your writing great on this page?

Week 8 — Day 3

Here is an account of everyday life by Seth, an eight year old boy who lives in Ancient Egypt. Read the text, then copy it out underneath.

I live with my family in a mud-brick house. Only rich children go to school. Instead, I work in the fields by the Nile with my dad, learning how to become a farmer. I play lots of fun games with my friends — my favourite game is marbles.

How did copying out this paragraph go?

Week 8 — Day 4

Read the information about the pyramids in Egypt below, then copy it out neatly.

The pyramids were burial places for the pharaohs. Hidden deep within were chambers full of treasure, with fiendish traps to keep robbers out. The Great Pyramid of Giza is the largest pyramid. It took thousands of workers over 20 years to build.

How well did you copy out this information?

Week 8 — Day 5

Here is a news report about the curse of the pharaohs. Read the article, then copy it out neatly underneath.

Pharaoh's Curse Strikes Archaeologist!

The curse of the pharaohs, which is rumoured to be cast upon anyone who disturbs an Ancient Egyptian mummy, struck again last night. Lord Carnarvon, who helped to discover the tomb of King Tutankhamun, has mysteriously died.

Was your handwriting brilliant on this page?

Week 9 — Day 1

All the words below end in either 'sure' or 'ture'.
Copy them out three times.

enclosure

exposure

insure

pleasure

treasure

adventure

capture

fracture

furniture

moisture

nature

picture

Was your handwriting superb on this page?

Week 9 — Day 2

The sentences below contain more words ending with 'sure' and 'ture'. Have a go at copying them out.

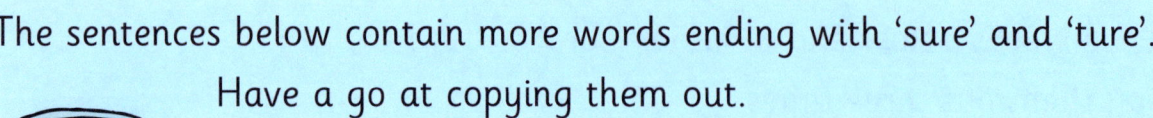

It was difficult to measure the goldfish.

The huge creature loomed over the little house.

In the summer holidays, I have more leisure time.

Laila thinks she is mature for her age.

As time ran out, the pressure began to rise.

During the ride, Ali's bike got a puncture.

Did you copy out these sentences neatly?

Week 9 — Day 3

Copy out each of these sentences on the lines below.

The horse, which was extremely scared of water, had to be carried by its owner.

The detective, despite having all the clues, still wasn't sure who the criminal was.

Gary, who has a long neck, had an accident.

Ada, who loves dogs, adopted a puppy.

How did you find copying these sentences?

Week 9 — Day 4

Read the limerick below, then copy it out.

There was a Young Lady of Bute,

Who played on a silver-gilt flute;

She played several jigs,

To her uncle's white pigs,

The amusing Young Lady of Bute.

by Edward Lear

How did you get on with copying this limerick?

Week 9 — Day 5

Here is some information about Mary Read, a female pirate. Read the passage, then copy it out underneath.

Mary Read was disguised as a boy when she was a child. When she grew up she pretended to be a man to work as a sailor and a soldier. Later on she became a pirate with a fearsome reputation. She fought beside Anne Bonny, another famous female pirate.

Was your pirate paragraph written perfectly?

Week 10 — Day 1

The 'uh' sound can be spelt 'ou'. The twelve words below contain examples of this. Copy each word out three times.

country

couple

courage

cousin

double

enough

nourish

rough

touch

tough

trouble

young

Did you copy out these words neatly?

Week 10 — Day 2

Here are some sentences containing words with prefixes.
Have a go at copying them out.

After the ride, Douglas dismounted his horse.

My younger sister misplaced her bag.

Toby has an inability to stay still for long.

Nadiya felt discouraged when she lost the race.

Everyone mistook Anna for her twin.

The incredible flower flourished in the greenhouse.

How did you find copying these sentences?

Week 10 — Day 3

Read this extract from 'Alice's Adventures in Wonderland' by Lewis Carroll. Then, copy it out neatly.

Alice thought she had never seen such a curious croquet-ground in her life; it was all ridges and furrows; the balls were live hedgehogs, the mallets live flamingoes, and the soldiers had to double themselves up and stand on their hands and feet, to make the arches.

Was your handwriting wonderful on this page?

Week 10 — Day 4

Here is some information about hedgehog hibernation. Copy out the sentences.

Hedgehogs hibernate in the winter to save energy.

Their heartbeat and breathing slow down.

They come out of hibernation as the temperature increases and their fat reserves start to run low.

Hedgehogs lose a lot of weight during hibernation.

When they wake, they are weak and confused.

Could you copy these hedgehog facts neatly?

Week 10 — Day 5

Read these instructions about how to build a hedgehog house. Copy them out neatly below.

First, carefully cut air vents and an entrance into a large plastic box. Next, put some straw, leaves or grass inside the box. Put the box near a hedge, then cover the top with a plastic sheet camouflaged with twigs and dry leaves. Wait for a hedgehog to decide it looks cosy.

How well did you copy these instructions?

Week 11 — Day 1

> Copy each of these words three times across the page.

vision

mansion

erosion

division

invasion

confusion

decision

collision

television

illusion

diversion

extension

How neatly did you write these words?

Week 11 — Day 2

Copy these sentences which contain words with prefixes.

There is a type of tiny jellyfish that is immortal.

Rodney had to redo his illegible homework.

When I returned, I found my room redecorated.

 Some people say that nothing is impossible.

I admitted that putting ice skates on a bird was immature and irresponsible.

How did you get on with these sentences?

Week 11 — Day 3

Copy this extract from The Railway Children, by Edith Nesbit.

Next moment a train had rushed out of the tunnel with a shriek and a snort, and had slid noisily past them. They felt the rush of its passing, and the pebbles on the line jumped and rattled under it as it went by. "Oh!" said Roberta, drawing a long breath; "it was like a great dragon tearing by."

Week 11 — Day 4

Neatly copy the first six lines of From a Railway Carriage, by Robert Louis Stevenson.

Faster than fairies, faster than witches,

Bridges and houses, hedges and ditches;

And charging along like troops in a battle,

All through the meadows the horses and cattle:

All of the sights of the hill and the plain

Fly as thick as driving rain.

How neatly were you able to copy these lines?

Week 11 — Day 5

Copy this paragraph about trains on the lines below.

In the early 1800s, the first steam trains were invented. Although they went at less than 10 mph, people were scared of travelling on them because they thought they wouldn't be able to breathe at such speeds. Today, people happily travel on electric trains at speeds of over 200 mph.

Did you manage to copy this paragraph neatly?

Week 12 — Day 1

Copy out the twelve adjectives ending in 'ous' twice.

courteous

dangerous

enormous

humorous

mountainous

obvious

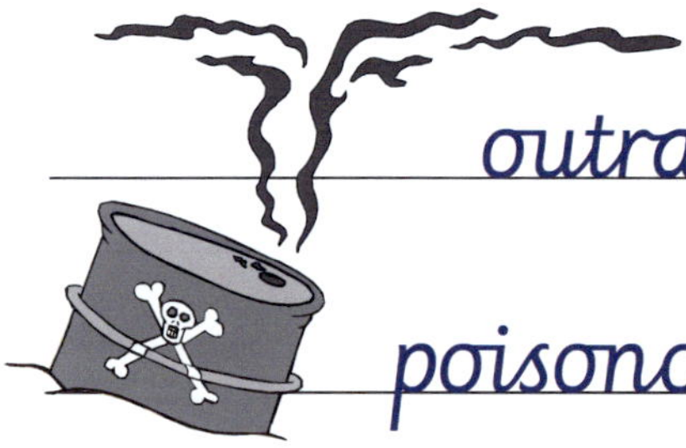

outrageous

poisonous

spontaneous

tremendous

various

vigorous

Was your handwriting tremend<u>ous</u> on this page?

Week 12 — Day 2

Here are some sentences containing adjectives that end in 'ous'. Copy them out neatly.

The witch had a hideous, cackling laugh.

Rowan wants to be a famous actor.

Josie was jealous of her sister's doll.

Colin was curious about everything.

My grandmother is extremely glamorous.

"Are you serious?" Obasi asked Hannah, smiling.

How did you get on with these sentences?

Week 12 — Day 3

A simile makes descriptions more interesting by comparing one thing to another. Copy out these examples.

The shark had a head like a hammer.

Her eyelashes are like butterflies, fluttering gently.

 Nat ran as fast as a dog chasing a rabbit.

His lip quivered like a flickering candle flame.

The waves tossed like a wriggling snake.

Erin danced as gracefully as a ballerina.

Was your writing as beautiful as a painting?

Week 12 — Day 4

An acrostic is a poem where the first letter of each line spells out a word. Read and copy out this acrostic poem about spring.

Sunlight dances across opening flowers,

Plants wake, flourishing in April showers.

Raindrops glisten on the window pane,

Indoors, children hope for sunshine again.

New life emerges, lambs frolic and play,

Grey skies dissolve as winter fades away.

How did copying out this poem go?

Week 12 — Day 5

Read the passage below about the history of April Fools' day. Then, copy it out underneath.

The origin of April Fools' day is unclear. It has been connected to a Roman festival of pranks. Others think it started when the new year moved from the end of March to January 1st. Those who continued to celebrate the old day were called 'April fools'.

Was your handwriting fantastic on this page?